D0309404

Dumfries and Galloway Libraries, Information and Archives

This item is to be returned on or before the last date
shown below.

ALK

2 2 MAY 2015 TH
UTH ≥ SCD.

- 8 NOV 2018

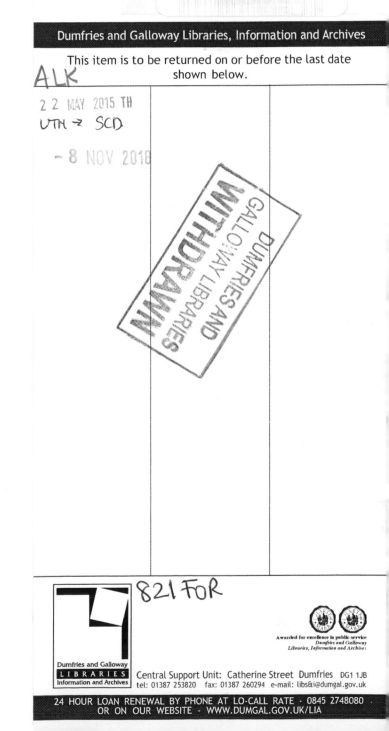

821 FoR

Dumfries and Galloway
LIBRARIES
Information and Archives

Awarded for excellence in public service
Dumfries and Galloway
Libraries, Information and Archives

Central Support Unit: Catherine Street Dumfries DG1 1JB
tel: 01387 253820   fax: 01387 260294 e-mail: libs&i@dumgal.gov.uk

24 HOUR LOAN RENEWAL BY PHONE AT LO-CALL RATE · 0845 2748080
OR ON OUR WEBSITE · WWW.DUMGAL.GOV.UK/LIA

FEAR OF THUNDER

RD
000958 82/
FOR

FEAR OF THUNDER

Andrew Forster

FlambardPress

First published in Great Britain in 2007 by Flambard Press
Stable Cottage, East Fourstones, Hexham NE47 5DX
www.flambardpress.co.uk

Typeset by BookType
Cover artwork © Andrew Foley
Cover Design by Gainford Design Associates
Printed in Great Britain by Cromwell Press, Trowbridge, Wiltshire

A CIP catalogue record for this book
is available from the British Library.
ISBN 978-1-873-226-94-0

Copyright © Andrew Forster 2007
All rights reserved.
Andrew Forster has exerted his moral rights in accordance
with the Copyright, Designs and Patents Act of 1988.

Flambard Press wishes to thank Arts Council England
for its financial support.

Flambard Press is a member of Inpress,
and of Independent Northern Publishers.

Mixed Sources
Product group from well-managed
forests and other controlled sources
www.fsc.org Cert no. TT-COC-2082
© 1996 Forest Stewardship Council
FSC

For Amanda

Acknowledgements

Thanks are due to the editors of the following magazines and anthologies, where some of these poems, or versions of them, first appeared: *Nerve, Cencrastus, Deliberately Thirsty, Lines Review, Poetry Nottingham, Obsessed with Pipework, Markings, Smiths Knoll, The Red Wheelbarrow, Poetry Scotland, The Eildon Tree, Southfields, West Coast Magazine, Acumen, Spectrum, Envoi, Edinburgh: An Intimate City, '. . . formally quite messy'* (Flarestack).

Some of these poems also appeared in 'Locked Gardens', a poetry card published by the School of Poets in 1997.

'Radnoti's Notebook' was commended by the judges of the 2003 Bridport Prize and published in the subsequent anthology.

Thanks also to the Scottish Arts Council for Writers' Bursaries in 1998 and 2002 to buy time during which some of these poems were written.

Last but not least, special thanks to Vicki Feaver and Mario Relich for their invaluable help in shaping this collection, and to Amanda Hunter, for everything.

Contents

1

Fear of Thunder

When Grandma heard thunder's first throaty murmur
she threw down her duster, or let dishes clatter in the sink,
grabbed Dad's hand and ran to the foot of the stairs.
Protected from the storm by a windowless door
she sang him *Blue Moon* in a trembling voice,
trying to drown the dark rumble,
holding him like a comfort blanket.

On August afternoons I tried to keep up
with Dad's hurried stride, as he trembled
at every truck that ran over a hole,
and scanned the sky for signs that only he could see.

When thunder rolled, Mum –
haunted by the fear that haunted him
and determined I wouldn't inherit it –
opened the door, set down chairs, letting lightning
show us X-rays of our narrow lawn.
We followed the storm across the sky,
measuring its distance by counting seconds

between lightning and thunder. Dad washed dishes,
the flashes revealing each bone of his face
with sudden, acrid clarity.

Black Beauty

If she couldn't play the game she wanted
she wouldn't play: just sat on the kerb,
skin like alabaster, smoky eyes
staring beyond the cramped brick terraces.

The first on the street with a colour TV,
she wouldn't allow me in her house
but let me watch *Black Beauty* through the window,
a drift of greens and reds that made no sense.

Afterwards, she played the horse, with me
the stumbling stable boy trying to catch her,
dark mane flying as she galloped through
the open field of the cul-de-sac.

Globetrotting

The youngest in a far-flung family,
her life was a parade of weddings,
engagement parties and week-long trips
to see sisters and brothers.
Names like *Skipsey*, *Kilwinning* and *Cowdenbeath*
slipped off her tongue as easily
as reciting characters from a Disney cartoon.

My world was marbles, hide-and-seek
and a once-a-week bus ride into town.
I asked her once if Scotland was over the sea
and she shook her head in disbelief
so I sat on the pavement and prodded
the quiet tarmac with a twig,
imagining the strangeness of anywhere but here.

Grandma's Gift

An urgent call to a neighbour's phone
hauled my Dad into a rainy March morning.
Returning, he told us Grandma had died.
He tied my shoelaces, ready for school,
while Mum cried and blamed in the kitchen's fierce light.

Last Christmas Eve, Grandma said
I should be seen and not heard. She scowled
when I poked my eye with the corner
of the sitting-room rug and reached
to her for comfort, tears streaming down my cheeks.

On Christmas morning her proud parcel
was an orange plastic truck, no bigger
than my hand, loaded with a plain white hankie.
It didn't compare with *Subbuteo*
from Uncle Bob, or Auntie Rita's *Colditz*.

I wondered why, when Grandma saw my mouth
drop at the sight of these heaped delights,
her awkward fingers scrabbled in her purse
to finally offer me a penny.
After all, what could you buy with it?

Brothers

Saddled with you for the afternoon, me and Paul
ambled across the threadbare field to the bus stop,
talking over Sheffield Wednesday's chances in the Cup
while you skipped beside us in your ridiculous tank-top,
spouting six-year-old views on Rotherham United.

Suddenly you froze, said you hadn't any bus fare.
I sighed, said you should go and ask Mum
and while you windmilled home I looked at Paul.
His smile, like mine, said I was nine and he was ten
and we must stroll the town, doing what grown-ups do.

As a bus crested the hill we chased Olympic Gold.
Looking back I saw you spring towards the gate,
your hand holding out what must have been a coin.
I ran on, unable to close the distance I'd set in motion.

At the Circus with My Brother

When Mother drew the tickets from her purse
I forgot you were only my younger brother.
Equals for the evening, we marched
into the world of posters plastered
in shop windows all over town:
clowns, jugglers, animals we'd only seen
on *Daktari*, in black-and-white.
My eyes grew wider with each drum-rolled wonder

but your face darkened as the night unfurled.
When the elephants stomped out to a fanfare
of applause, golden head-dresses glittering,
trunks like rope-swings, you started to cry.
It was only then I noticed the way
they shambled through sawdust
at the shot of the whip, shaking their heads,
not understanding how they arrived here.

The Pog

On one knee in the corner by the hedge
Mr Rockett chiselled the pog from tarmac,
a few safe adult strides from cars
reversing into the cul-de-sac.

Earlier he'd shouted warnings
while we crouched in the road, flicking marbles
at the long low pog beneath the kerb
that could hold a hundred easily.

He dropped two marbles in the hole he'd made
then pushed himself up, softly massaging
the small of his back. Noticing my frown,
he bent to double the size of the pog.

How could I tell him it wouldn't be enough?
I wanted a pog for *cats' eyes*, *trapped twists*,
silver bombers: flames suspended in glass,
flickering against the dirty brick terrace.

Grades

The hottest August in sixteen years
when I tore off my school-tie for good:
wrung-out, dried-up, all I bothered to do
was read *Catch-22* and *The Ginger Man*
in a deckchair on the yellowing lawn.

At last the envelope dropped on the carpet,
with the cramped address in my own writing,
the computer-generated slip it contained
trembling in the tightness of my grip,
useless as a handful of cold ash.

In the kitchen my mother settled bread
on a cooling rack. I read the results
as if they could be declared and forgotten.
If she was to tell me she expected more
it wasn't more than I expected myself.

'What will you do now?' she asked,
standing relaxed in the growing heat.
I searched for an answer in the lino's pattern
but light through the window strafed the floor
and reflected the question back to me.

Mother, Diving

The high diving board at the open-air pool
taunted my mother like a tongue. While young boys
leapt from the first board, clenched like stones,
she held herself in by the pool-rail.
Then one day she just shrugged off the shallows,
strode like Johnny Weismuller to the deep end.
I had no idea what she was climbing towards
but she reached the top, balanced above
the craning necks, and stretched. A short run
and she sprang into the charged air,
making new shapes for herself: twisting
and turning like a dolphin, plunging into water –
a guillemot, sending out relentless waves
that will keep on nudging me off balance.

Jason

Jason, the neighbour's Yorkshire terrier
would sit, sharp-eared, awaiting an order
before tonguing crumbs from an offered palm.
'The best-natured dog in the world.'
But when I nipped next door, full of the thought
of *Ker-Plunk* or *Mousetrap*, his rat-like scurry
and low growl sent me crashing into chairs,
needle-teeth locked around my ankle.

Returning from college years later,
I was city-wise, head tumbled with theories,
dropping names like encyclopaedias,
my mellow glow of sophistication
lighting the narrow terraces.
Jason, patchy-haired, grey bearded,
shambled towards me, spongy damp gums
clamping my ankles, refusing to let go.

2

An East Lothian Farm

She sips broth, alone at the table,
her foot tapping the stone-flagged floor,
eyes prickly-red from before-dawn rising:
feeling her way across the courtyard
to coax milk from reluctant udders;
the blundering flutter-squawk of chickens
pecking her hands as she delves into a sack
to whirl blizzards of corn over cobbles.

Down the corridor, in the family room,
the farmer is joking, something about
a farmhand and a teat. The laughter echoes
nights before her parents sent her here.
Beside her bowl the *Daily Sketch* is open
at an advert: an aeroplane
flying towards a giant kangaroo.
*'Emigrate to Australia. Ten Pounds
Only.'* A sewing box full of coins
will take her up, up, away from all this.

The Parlour

She keeps the room locked, but each morning
her duster glosses the stately darkness
of the mahogany table and chairs;
it shines the banquet of china, holding
fragile expectation behind the bureau's glass;
it dances lightly across the piano
she's never learned to play; and caresses
the rows of silver-framed photographs
preserving her Claudette Colbert loveliness.

If her grandson peeks in from the rosebed
through the gap between the folds of lace
her stare will tumble him across the lawn.
Nothing must disturb this church-like stillness.
Nothing must shatter the spell of midnight's pianist
whose elegant rhapsodies whisk her
shadow-self towards each rose-tinted dawn.

Choices

When they gave him a choice he chose the air force.
I'd rather be above them than have them above me.

On first-leave he rapped the door formally,
waited in a too-big uniform with polished buttons,
grinning shyly like a schoolboy forced to wear a tie
presenting himself to the *ooh's* and *aah's* of family.

When he speaks now of bases, compasses, charts
(but never of flights through darkness shot with fire)
after a while his words go missing, lost in a glassy stare.

His uniformed grin is framed on his sideboard
beside a balsa wood Sunderland Flying Boat
and a silver carriage clock with a plaque, engraved,
from Jenkins Engineering, the firm
that gave him orders when the war was done.
He could have risen through their ranks
but promotion meant travel and he refused to fly.

A Story

Nineteen thirty-eight, it must have been.
Walking on the beach at North Berwick.
The sun on Bass Rock. Everybody stared
at Sheila on my arm.

When Paul was born I was out of action.
Bullet in the shoulder.
The Sergeant-Major marched up the ward.
Robinson. Gift of a son.
When he'd gone I heard Joe, my pal,
hadn't made it.

Afterwards I carried samples of peanuts
around the coast, used to add up my orders
on the train journey home.
Paul would be in bed,
dinner in the oven.

Paul sent us a card from South Africa.
It showed skyscrapers round Table Mountain.
He drew an arrow, pointing to a window,
wrote – My office.
He was going to send us the air-fare
so we could visit. Sheila couldn't manage
the journey now.

Last year he came over.
Threw us a party, for our fiftieth anniversary.
You should have seen him tip the waiters.
He wants to buy us a bigger house.
It's an investment really, in case he wants
to move back after we're gone.

A Woman Sewing

after the painting by Vilhelm Hammershoi

Dressed in mourning, hair harshly knotted,
she bends over her labours, deft fingers
working needle through cloth. Late daylight
paints the window's silhouette on floorboards.
White curtains framing the window glow
like hope but the oak door remains shut.
There may be laughter from the street outside
reminding her of still-born dreams,
but she stays in this room:
table, chair and sewing her only company.

As night crawls into your house, you draw
the curtains, dye the room with electric light.
Your hands once tried to capture life
in watercoloured moments, but now
they cook for your expectant children.
You stopped renewing paints and brushes.
The easel broods in the loft like a secret.
Rising to clear the evening's casual debris
your glance skims the print above the fireplace
of a woman sewing and a shut door.

In the Evening

Clothes are ironed, folded, filed away.
The mantelpiece and coffee table
are polished to a mirror, the carpet
so clean you could eat off it,
and cushions sit plump on the new suite –
like the one she sighed at in showrooms
when money was swallowed by growing boys.

He watches *Strike it Rich*, belching laughter,
checks the time before night shift,
glances across. She's still there
considering rambling roses on wallpaper
and if the curtains match. He stands,
stretches, takes neatly packaged sandwiches
from the kitchen and coat from the hall.
A peck on the cheek and he's gone. What's left
for her now? She could phone the boys,
hear about jobs, intoxicate herself
on their sparkling lives. It may be enough.

In the attic of her memory, a photograph,
black and white: Trafalgar Square, 1961,
her coat out of *On the Road*, his hair
combed to a blade; smalltowners
out of their depth, drowning in the flood
of pigeons, but they stood close, held hands,
vice-like, all the courage they needed.

Frames

If her evening were a movie, she thinks
it would have some meaning. This aching yawn,
feeling wrung out like a windowcleaner's cloth,
fingers doodling on the TV remote control,
would establish her as a character.

This drab sofa would be vivid onscreen,
plain walls could be filtered to sepia.
A soundtrack would tint the mood: something upbeat,
maybe sixties soul, to add an ironic rhythm,
even a mournful guitar adagio

would make her poignant, a tragic heroine.
In a movie, this would be a prelude to a plot.

Choosing to Disappear

It's just on odd mornings, at first.
His house is glossed by a different light.
Lines and edges sharpen. Chairs, tables,
drawers stand free of familiarity,
become mere objects on display.
His daughter's laughter, pearls tinkling,
is a memory he's trying to place.
His son has a face like the face
in the mirror whose contours he touches
as if testing a blade. And this woman,
his wife, her intimate smile speeds
his breathing, creeps from his skin like dew.
He shrugs it off with a routine
he wears like a suit, but it drips
into his consciousness, this feeling,
like a leaking pipe into a basin.

More and more he lingers
at chance meetings with strangers,
devours tiny details of other lives,
imagines being immersed in them
like a second skin, as if this would stop
his being outside himself, disbelieving
the life he lives, not remembering
how he arrived here. So he starts
a game, like a secret passion
for chocolate, something to sweeten
the days, make them easier to swallow:
money sliced off the joint account,
squirreled in a drawer beneath socks
and underwear, beside bus timetables
to places he's never been, or where
he spent holidays that fit like a glove.

From time to time his family notice
him looking at them without seeing,
but brush it away like mud trailed in a kitchen.
They're too caught up by their rush of days.
He does what he should, doesn't interfere,
so they carry his sometimes-silences
like a river grasping a fallen branch.
The kids slip into sleep warmed
by his stories of Narnia, oblivious
to his popping out to the late-night shop
and when he shoves the wad of notes
into his pocket, it means nothing:
just the game gone one stage further.
He checks that milk is all they need,
not sure why his token kiss lingers
on his wife's cheek, and he leaves.

She doesn't look at the time at first,
trying to piece together
a jigsaw-puzzle TV drama
and when all pieces are fixed in place
she curses the friends he must have met
and sips black coffee, impatience
measured by the hands of the clock.
Later, or the next day, she will look
for a trail on the rain-washed street:
check with the shopkeeper, question
staff at the local bar, phone around
unlikely acquaintances, consider the police
and that's it. There isn't an ending.
Just a litre of milk left behind
on a 305 bus, found
by a puzzled driver, about to go home.

Leaving

The men from the council curse
the three flights of stairs
as they manoeuvre furniture
to cart it to the landfill site:
a couch weeping foam, dressing table,
a dismantled double-bed.

She stares down through the window
at neighbours' children
acting half-understood battles
on the grass verge
while she waits for the ambulance
to take her to the nursing home.

A few clothes in a suitcase
buckled with the weight of holidays past.
Not much else worth taking.
A box filled for the charity shop:
dolls in shabby national costume,
a *Tower of London* snowstorm.

All she wants is the letter –
on parchment with a Royal Crest –
informing her that her husband's
missing in action: sweat-stained,
tearing at the folds, as if touch
could erase meaning.

3

The Carved Head

Her Masai profile sculpted from ebony,
forehead scarred from a fall into some packing crate;
a present from an uncle, a souvenir
from a past he wished to clear away,
part of the debris of his failed marriage,
but her lips keep silence, somehow graceful.

I've always liked her in an unthinking way:
a comforting weight in my luggage,
the heavy wood a perfect bookend,
her presence on a shelf or sideboard
transforming anonymous rooms into homes.

You accepted her presence immediately,
matching it with paintings, rugs and tapestries.
Perhaps it's no surprise that the psychic
you saw from curiosity should detect her.
He said she missed foliage, craved greenery
so we traipsed in a jungle of aspidistras.

Raindance

With yellow oilskins and blue galoshes
wrapped around your business suit,
you're dressed for a term on an oil-rig,
not a short walk along George Street.

But this is no quenching, diamond cloudburst.
It's a rain with self-confidence. It darkens
the faces of offices, dribbles
over gutter-lips, pooling on pavements.

While others hurry past, briefcases
and newspapers forming clumsy umbrellas,
the rain slides off you, releasing
something you keep just below the surface.

Navigating to the largest puddles
you stamp with both feet, splashing the street
with dark waves, laughing at the alchemy
as streetlamps transform rain to gold.

On Yellowcraigs Beach

Sand glitters around our feet.
We slope towards the breaking wall of the sea.
A heron cranes its neck, shocked by the sky.
Jellyfish spatter the beach.

I crouch on sandstone,
trying to place the smell of blistering wrack,
fingers of heat drumming my neck.
You scrabble for a witchstone
in a mosaic of pebbles.

Pines on the cliff are a memory
of emerald. Mist burns off leaves.
This could be South America, not here
in this country defined by drizzle.
The sun hands down its Midas touch,
ignites the sand.

You straighten, hold the stone disc high.
Light pierces the central hole
as through a camera eye, shuttered
by your charged fingers.

Power Failure

Somewhere the storm has severed a cable, and we
are in darkness. Emergency lines are busy
and the night screams *This will last some time*

so we scrabble in the cupboards for candles,
woollen jumpers, settle down to weather it out.
I try to read by soft flame but it's no use:

words flicker in and out of shadows at random
and, in any case, the mounting screech of wind
delivering echoes of distant crashes, shatters

my concentration, crams my head with disasters.
I prowl the floor, snatch aside the curtain,
peer into shifting blackness to check the car

is still there. You smile at my agitation
and cross to the kitchen for a glass of water.
The sultry dance of the candle's flame

abandons your face, but as you bend once more
into the spill of light, you are revealed again
in fragments, with a fresh perspective:

a new angle to your jaw, golden sheen
on your cheek, the red in the brown of your hair.
These things about you I haven't seen before.

Ten years are built around us, but each
ordeal we face you surprise me, as new facets
of you, new depths, rise to the light.

After leaving you at the airport . . .

I'm driving home, eyes sore from a 3:30 start,
through the grainy darkness of a black-and-white movie.
You're flying towards a time-lapse: five hours
refunded on arrival. For two weeks
I'll imagine your clear summer afternoon
as I settle for a screeching December night.

The day feels upside-down. It's only 6 a.m.
but cars and lorries tear up the silence.
I take the wrong lane at South Gyle roundabout
and I'm pulled into the City, past sleeping shops and houses.
I grit my teeth. No suitable place to turn around.

Nothing for it but to pass through the centre,
look forward to the calm on the other side.

Moon Over Cullen Bay

Nestled in coat and scarf, I pick my way
to the brushed velvet of a beach
far north of my own.
The wind whips laments from withered thistles
and lashes a disgruntled murmur
from the not-quite-invisible sea.

All day my landscape is a noticeboard
above a desk, and now, in the dark
I am looking for a way to love
this coastline where I have dropped
like a pebble from a child's hand.

The moon is amazing:
a white featureless face
with blue rumours of age
just beneath the skin.
Still, like mercury trailing on black oil,
it casts its net on the water.

I wish you could see this with me.

Shadows

Your voice is a husk, captured
from breath you struggle to draw.
You're getting worse.

The doctor clipped the X-rays to the light,
showed a bright grotto, empty of shadows
but his brow furrowed, and the drumming
of his fingers beat out other possibilities:
pleurisy, pneumonia . . .
He only agreed to send you home
with the promise of feet-up, daytime TV
and staying in touch.

I fuss around you with blankets, pillows,
scatter words of encouragement
but I'm patronising you and we know it.

When you are settled I walk to the window
and stare at winter rain as though the future
is patterned in its heavy curtain:
fearing the worst but wanting to know.

Colours

Your smile crumples as you step back
to stare at the custard yellow you carefully diluted
and swept on the walls in confident arcs.
It's not how you imagined it,
the colours in your head too rich
for the light of East Coast Scotland.

Scarlets, oranges, deep deep greens
more suited to the summer glare
of your Southern Cape, which shimmers
on the highways, bubbling tarmac;
houses, in confident isolation, are bleached
to a blank canvas against the sky;
cardboard-strewn streets are scoured
and sleeveless strollers are thrown into sharp silhouettes
as the light stretches over white, white sand
to a horizon more distant than imagination.

Here the light is bed-ridden,
crippled by oaks, sycamores
and the voracious huddle of buildings.
Your colours clutter the space, trapping you.

Chance

This time it's the cards, dealt in a neat circle.
You'll pray for the Empress's smile, probe the pattern.
Last night you drew runes from a velvet bag.
Whenever chance slaps you, you search for a hint
that this casual assault will cease, and time
will rub some balm on the stinging fingerprints.

We know that I think the stars are an accident,
a beautiful chaos we impose our myths on.
The psychic at the fair was a shrewd observer.
He knew your friend was deaf in one ear by the slight
inclination of her head when you spoke.

But my sweeping dismissal won't release
the white set of your lips, the tight clench of grief.

Distances

I'm startled from a dream of walking alone
on a damp lane that might have been on Islay
where we haven't been for fifteen years.
The engine of a car revving towards me
slowly softens to the drone of a printer.
You are a cold absence beside me.
The room's warm blackness is cut
by the edge of light beneath the door.
My watch glows 3 a.m. I stumble towards you,
screwing my eyes against the light
Hunched over the keyboard, you don't look up.
I'm surprised to see the words on the screen
are written in a language I understand.

Paths

There's no point in talking further.
We only think we're in this room
pushing half-eaten meals around our plates.
We're standing on opposing sides
of that West Coast loch from years ago.
Our words fall short of each other like
hurled stones dropping into grey water
disappearing without a ripple.

You are searching the gorse for a hint
of a path to take you somewhere
as yet unknown: still real to you as a dream
you've not quite woken from, its traces
suggesting a smile on your lips.

I'm trying to get back to our cabin
beside the oak: from tangled sheets
on a makeshift bed, we gazed outside
at rows of finches perched like a jury,
laughed and wondered what their verdict would be.

The Horses

Our car coughs into the scrapyard, burning oil
smoking into the stillness of the lane.
You sign the document and that's it –
no point holding onto something that's dying.

Under a shifting roof of cloud we trudge
to the road. Chestnuts, elms and sycamores
strain with the weight of leaves, and rosebay
withers, its purple flowers yellowing

at the edges like pages of an old book.
Heading for the bus stop you turn, suggest
a walk. I shrug and we take the coastal path.
The harbour is deserted: a single boat,

paint flaking, is rocked on the water,
the empty clank of its rigging keeping time
with a half-hearted breeze. A gull takes off
from the crumbling wall with a clatter of wings.

Leaving the road, we climb down through gorse
to the beach. The clouds make space so the sun
can improvise something upbeat on my neck.
You quicken your pace and we sit on the sand.

The tide is in. Not far from the water's edge
the land must shelve, as the sea is suddenly
deeper. Two horses splash past us,
water lapping at their torsos. Their riders

lean back in their saddles, angling their boots clear.
The sun strokes the horses' flanks, picking out
shades of chestnut as they pull their freedom
from the sea's grasp, then slap their hooves

down again, moving on, shaking their manes,
showering silver spray into the air.
The riders' laughter hangs in the afternoon
as they let themselves be carried forward.

4

Horizons

He wouldn't let the cooling towers and factories
of Rotherham's horizon restrict his view.
Even at sixteen, a dozen city-maps were printed
on his memory. On my first trip to London
he waited for me to come up from the Underground
to show me streetlights paving the Strand with gold.

A year later, he lived in a Birmingham suburb:
Vauxhall in the drive, listening to the radio
for Chelsea's results with a distance in his eyes.
Just a temporary hitch and no surprise
he went back to London,
but a West End loft *and* a pad in New York.

Once, on Westminster Bridge, while I struggled to keep up
he told me how his father, a surgeon (famous
in Rotherham), newly-qualified and penniless,
worked his passage from Bombay in 1948.
'My father's story is what I think with,' he said
pausing, his gaze following lights down the Thames.

Critical

for Stephen

Morphine has glazed your eyes into slivers
of black porcelain. The tube draining your lung
traps your right arm to the hospital bed
but in cracked movements your left hand shifts
the oxygen mask and you tell the story.

A summer Sunday's biking, away from the family,
you misjudged the bend at *The Cat and Fiddle*,
fifth this month in that peaceful spot.
Your voice slithers to a standstill
then sputters back to life as you mutter
'Seven ribs,' slapped again by the closeness of the call.

A nurse checks the charts, asks, in a cheerful tone
if you've given up the motorbike.
You shake your head firmly, leaving no doubt.
In this critical moment you find fluent movement
somewhere inside that refuses to be broken.

Failing

As I point to the *Ladies*, I ask you, Mother,
beneath the hearing of the lounging waiters,
if you can reach it on your own.
'No problem,' you say, and begin to cross the bar.
Sunlight through glass walls coats the pine floor
but you shuffle along, hands held out
in slight defence, adjusting your path
as you almost hit each obstacle.

Earlier in the supermarket
you lowered your face to read labels
like a chemist at a microscope
and asked the girl at the checkout, quietly,
if the note you offered was a five or a ten.

I'm shocked at the sight of you, and I see
how comfortable I've become
with the miles that separate us, aware
of the milky pearls blurring your sight
only through your casual remarks on the phone
about your eyes not being what they were.

You reach the top of the stairs.
Embarrassed, your fingers tighten
around the handrail, as your foot slides
to the silver runner on the step
to test its edge. I don't think

your understatement was just for my benefit.
Both of us have been blind to reality.

A Friend in Hospital

I imagine her, shocked by the suddenness
of a green ward, gazing at others
who pace the tiled floors in decreasing
circles, clutch tatters of identity
like a photograph or purse.
Her breath catches on the word *bulimic*.

It's the latest in a list of illnesses
my friends are slipping into.
It could be my age. At forty-three
I like to think my eyes are open
to what is really there.
I finally understand
my mother's silent carpet-stare
when I asked my childhood questions
about Aunt Jean's long holidays.

Dolphins in the Moray Firth

1. Searching

I don't know how long this will last: the weekly train
up and down the country; evenings in this winter-quiet
hotel, trying to clear my head to read or phone home
with little to tell but needing the anchor of the open-line.
I'm the only person in the dining room some nights,
talking to my reflection in the picture window.

Each morning the wind freezes my face as I wait
for the bus to coast me through Portknockie, Findochty,
Portessie: villages tumbling toward the dolomite teeth
lining the foam-flecked turmoil of the Firth.
Finally, the sleeping harbour of Buckie,
my temporary workplace, where the day is an aching blur
as I balance arguments, make decisions with fingers crossed.
Then back again through the salty darkness.

My colleagues tell me there are dolphins here. They come in
with the tide, in schools, to preen, loup and frolic,
mimicking strollers and beachcombers. In the daylight
I manage to snatch, I walk around Cullen Bay
and stare at the water's simmering hues, double-taking
at shifting shadows as I urge the surface to break.

2. Seeing

It's the final lap of my job here.
The end date is tangible as a silk ribbon.
Alex arrived yesterday
and I'm trying to put a rhythm
to the last six months, to order it:
a balance-sheet or confession,
present it to him like a baton.

Spring has stretched the days with the slow
determination of a tractor
ploughing a field and I am, in the end,
settling in a stride, beginning to warm
to these gorse-straggled crags, this broken coastline.
Each night now, before dinner,
I explore dips and crevices,
push my territory further, camera
around my shoulder for memory's sake.

Now, in the office, I'm on the phone,
another goodbye to tick off.
Alex scans papers with the saucer-eyed stare
of an unprepared student before an exam.
Suddenly, a glint outside
magnetizes his gaze, and his finger
trembles like a compass needle.

In the Firth a tug slouches.
In its wake there must be twenty dolphins.
They curve and twist into a youthful sky,
arch and descend, shatter the surface
in explosions of silver
and rise again in a glittering dance.

The Clock

It must have been elegant, this wooden clock.
A wedding gift, from someone left behind
at the two-sitting reception in Brown Street Club.
In the cavernous house on the Grove
and your widow's bungalow on the near side of town
it dissolved the years,
sat like the Sphinx on your mantel.

Now it sits on mine
but twisted hinges by the face
no longer hold protective glass,
hands move only when my hands move them
and it chimes for amusement at the turn of a spring.
I've talked about repairing it, this inheritance,
and I will, in time.

5

Horse Whisperer

They shouted for me
when their horses snorted, when restless
hooves traced circles in the earth
and shimmering muscles refused the plough.
My secret was a spongy tissue, pulled bloody
from the mouth of a just-born foal,
scented with rosemary, cinnamon,
a charm to draw the tender giants
to my hands.

They shouted for me
when their horses reared at burning straw
and eyes revolved in stately heads.
I would pull a frog's wishbone,
tainted by meat, from a pouch,
a new fear to fight the fear of fire,
so I could lead the horses,
like helpless children, to safety.

I swore I would protect
this legacy of whispers
but the tractor came over the fields
like a warning. I was the life-blood
no longer. From pulpits
I was scorned as demon and witch.
Pitchforks drove me from villages and farms.

My gifts were the tools of revenge.
A foul hex above a stable door
so a trusted stallion could be ridden
no more. Then I joined the stampede,
with others of my kind,
to countries far from our trade.

Still I miss them. Shire, Clydesdale, Suffolk.
The searing breath, glistening veins,
steady tread and the pride,
most of all the pride.

Film Noir

1.

He wears a Homburg, tipped forward,
a raincoat, stone-coloured, tightly-belted:
lights a cigarette beneath a sign
for an Adult Bar, reflections of its neon
swirling on the wet sidewalk.

He sees her legs first: sparkling silk,
rapier heels, emerging from the dark sedan.
She moves like the moon on water
but just for a second is still
and he exhales smoke on the screen

of her dark glasses. Her lips
pout in a half-question, then her arm
is grasped by a sober-suited man
with eyes like granite, and she's gone.
But our man has seen enough

to know how this will pan out. He knows
she will come to him. He knows it will end
with blood, money, perhaps with love.
It's inevitable as midnight, as dawn.
Winning or losing, it's all the same,

it's just a question of flicking away
a cigarette and moving forward.

2.

Different script, same plot: jazz-age improvisation.
Even the way he pours Jack Daniels
from a crystal decanter, his sudden pause
as he hands her the tumbler, is shot with meaning.
She'll play dumb for the first thirty minutes,
wait for the close-up, for the stranger in a homburg
to show if the face he wears is a mask.

Then she'll know if she can trust him
with nightly scenes in back-rooms along the strip.
Secrets are hers as she's a work of art,
a silent construction of gold, silk and paint
framed by limousines and satin restaurants.
All the complexities are still so simple:
this is deliberate black-and-white.

3.

It's raining, a steady grain flickering
through the scene. He's played this role so often
he exists simultaneously
in different episodes within the story.

He parks the car, turns up his raincoat collar
and he's already kneeling in the alley,
nose covered against the vegetable stench,
prodding the crumpled litter that used to be a man;

and he's shouldering into gilt-edged offices
behind casinos, hitting his head
against the well-dressed laughter of those
who don't recognise that this worn and faded plot

has only a fixed amount of time;
but the soundtrack at the closing credits
will not be the slam of a cell door,
just a car's engine settling into distance.

He pulls a notebook from his pocket.
One day soon he will break the pattern.

4.

What can they do, this woman and her stranger
when the plot that held them together
sputters to a standstill like a black sedan
running out of gas? When they're far away
from the body in the swimming pool,
the car sits by the highway like regretted words,
blood is rinsed away in a motel sink,
the money in the case is counted, stashed?

They'll try to settle for a leafy street,
hawk real estate and bake apple pies
but, type-cast, they'll soon become entangled
by the old script in a new location.

The past isn't erased with rolling credits
and raising of lights: it's a tired detective
snooping around palm trees in the afternoon
wondering why lamps around the pool still burn.

Radnotti's Notebook

It's the sort you can buy in a corner shop:
stapled, pages ruled into a squared grid,
like a child might use for elementary sums
or a gambler for calculating odds.

But in *this* one, in midnight moments stolen
from the dense, creaking shifts of nightmares
in the bunks around him, he composed
eclogues and 'postcards', with a stub-pencil,

with only the moon's white fingers clinging
to the sill of the one high window, as guide.
No corrections, no scribbles – a flowing script,
just two neat stars and a sharp arrow

to show the reordering of a stanza;
forced labours measured in smooth iambics
as if the challenge of his half-rhymed metre
let him leave the taut hammering of his nerves;

or as if he'd been encamped to witness.
The last poem was on the march, written
on a faded Cod Liver Oil label
and carefully gummed in the book.

And he took such care to see the book reached
beyond its threadbare confines, a request
for delivery to his friend Gyula
printed at the front (in four languages).

Miklos, I'm fairly sure, in your position:
starved, friends in the dust before dancing
briefly in the shock of machine-gun fire,
I wouldn't be worthy of poetry's demands.

Rescued from the pocket of his matted coat,
though brown with damp the book was well preserved.
Astonishing that, from such close range,
the burst of bullets missed it entirely.

Robert Graves in Deya

England is a crumpled first draft, long ago
tossed aside. He's a God here, thunder-voice
hurling locals down the tumble of paths
into the refuge of white-washed stone houses.
His family know his rhythms, not to disturb
pensive walks through almond groves, gnawing
a phrase, a line to resurrect the sacred.

Now he's enthroned on the terrace, beneath
the silver whisper of olive trees. He watches
the setting sun play its colourful drama
on the face of the Teix, his thoughts flooded
by rising tides of opinion and mounting costs.
An invitation to lecture in America
is buried in his pocket like a hook.

Robert Lowell on Marlborough Street

Between breakdowns, he looks down on Boston
from the upper windows of Marlborough Street.
With chandeliers sparkling and heavy drapes
to shut out the uninvited, it's the image
of his family home. He presides like a lion
at the head of the table as if,
when he laboured up the cemetery path
out of his mother's grey shadow,
he gave himself permission to shrug off
his country tweeds, come back to town
and be what she always wanted him to be.

After the guests, alone in his room, the bed
a shambles of ashtrays, books and letters,
he adjusts his glasses, smokes, scribbles
notes in margins, stripping back layers
of family history: the gravel-faced pilgrim;
a shadowy Governor; that solitary rider
hunting buffalo on the new frontier;
and the proud revolutionary, waving his flag
on cobbled streets. Turning page
after page, Lowell summons their spirits
like a shaman, shuffles his metres
to accept their stories as part of his own
in the frantic process of becoming.

Elizabeth Bishop at Outer Banks

At low tide she steps carefully on the sandflats,
her breathing settling to its own rhythm
in this still, open space at the centre
of a whirlwind of greyhound buses, taxis,
podiums, applause. How do you explain a poem?
It's like Robinson Crusoe back in England
asked to explain his *plucked fowl* of a parasol:
you survive, using the means at your disposal.

She pauses by the dunes, fearful of disturbing
nesting terns; looks at horsemint, gaillardia,
sturdy sea-oats fencing the dunes in,
preventing erosion – if she looks long enough
she might stumble on their secret.
She pencils notes but the wind is rising.

Suddenly there's the cry of a heron, pure,
beautiful. She turns to watch
the sure beat of its wings
carrying it to the distant ocean,
away from the flats where pools of water
turn to blood in the setting sunlight.

Fingal's Cave

The moan and crash of Atlantic swell
against basalt pipes would not let Mendelssohn go.
It resonated like a fever, a layered melancholy.
With a script for strings and woodwind
he tried to conjure the cavernous halls.

Musicians, touring the Hebrides, floated in
on platforms, scratched tunes to rebound
in bass echoes from broken black columns,
played the stalactitic roof like chimes

Turner too was drawn here. His charcoal scraped
a brisk image of the Great Face of Staffa
whose crooked mouth disconcerted with its chords.

6

Winter Night: Edinburgh

Night falls quickly as turning back a clock
but the City is alive with light.
Shops and cafés deny the darkness,
throw light at the street like baited hooks.
Offices spill workers onto pavements,
the yellow drip of lamps washing colour
from their faces as they pass beneath.
Cars, trapped in a magnetic flow, controlled
by coloured lights, thrust beams at the blackness.

It can be seen for miles, this Metropolis:
glowing orange like a prehistoric fire.

Aberlady

You can pass through without knowing it. A street
hugging the coast. The sleep of a postcard church
nursed by headstones. Fashionable cloisters
rub puritan townhouses the wrong way
and kitchen-garden cottages embarrass
the modern visions of architects. The doors of two hotels
yawn open, wait for golfers to finish the course.
The rest of the village staggers up past the school,
peters out in potato fields and caravan parks.

It's a base-camp, a bridge to the nature reserve
or a strand of beach littered with driftwood.
If you catch buses you might nod into
acquaintances, but most of us take cars,
disappear into the City as dawn gilds the church,
our absence vivid as September light,
and when we return we live our evenings
behind heavy curtains, while the street is loud
with the steady breath of the sea.

Kilspindie Bay

The tide has pulled the cloak from this landscape,
leaving a shell-studded crust of sand.
The sea is a distant, rubbed-out pencil-line.

Trees, stripped by saltwater diligence, are angled
on moss-soaked rocks, sculpted limbs suggesting speech
frozen on the verge of expression.

Plastic bottles, tossed over the sides of boats,
are scattered here and there like promises
but bleached labels hold no message.

A few gulls poke at tangles of wrack and kelp:
screams of frustration needle-scratch the silence,
and deliberate wings beat the sour sky.

There are sunken ships beneath the skin
of this bay, but only spindly masts
are visible, protruding like an old fence.

After the Storm

It's as if you've been asleep. The rain has stopped
and in the blustery, late afternoon light
you walk through a world that seems to have lost
its balance: tilted, slightly, on its axis.

The wood is a swamp. Oaks and maples, pale, naked,
grow from murky water, glisten in the dimness.
Sweet green air ripples the outer branches
but inside is still as a photograph
of a wood, the only movement a faint
mysterious dapple of rings on pools of water.

Beside the wood, the burn, in spate, wears clay
from its own banks, sweeps up branches which surge past
like figureheads torn from the prows of longboats.

Ahead of you, the burn has spilled over.
In the middle of a field, where shoots of corn flutter
limp as broken banners, a lake has formed,
opaque as an old mirror, reflecting nothing,
the wind lazily scratching its surface.

Two greylag geese waddle on the fringes,
jerky gazes taking in their new environment.
You watch as a cluster of tern paddle out
unflustered, as if it were always this way.

Walking Through Aberlady Bay: September

This afternoon, summer has made a late appearance.
A few cumulus clouds float like whales through the slow warmth
of the sky. Across the Forth the cranes and piers of Fife

are etched against the green and gold of sharp-lined fields.
I cross the shaky bridge into the Nature Reserve, away
from the bee-like drone of cars on the coastal road.

Greying gorse and crimson spears of sorrel guard the path;
withered thistles are coated with white seeds, as if
in a premonition of frost. Across the quiet golf-course

I trek up a final ridge to where sand scuttles beneath my feet
and the sea stretches before me. The sun projects
the pattern of waves on the sea-bed like a honeycomb

and picks out shades of brown in sand. This is as far
as rock and the tide will let me go: a sheltered space
against a sandstone cliff. A salt breeze combs my hair,

the sea stammers gently. Sandflies dance, starlings
dart like minnows. Somewhere in the distance,
a curlew repeats the same question over and over.

Snow on Portobello Beach

Through the bay window the sky swirls
with snow, obscuring the sea.
The two Annas, city-fresh,
stare open-mouthed, point out patterns
in the shifting haze. I turn away.
It's not an angel's frozen tears,
confetti, or time to drag out the sledge –
just a blurring of plans, a slow drive home
with flickering visibility.

But it's finished quickly as it began.
Sharp-edged February light re-forms
revealing sand mapped by melting white.
Anna and Anna shoot down the beach,
kick sand and snow into spray,
tear off scarves and brandish them
as they dance before the rolling waves.

Drumlanrig Forest

Hawthorn, horse-chestnut and ash are free
to climb, to let branches follow
the emerald-scented twists of imagination.

Light is fox-like, darting behind bracken
to nose out of the shifting spaces
between the whispering net of leaves.

Behind the silence the Nith cascades
wanting no more than to continue
the long course of its dreaming.

Here and there on the glistering banks
solitary fishermen bide their time
as lines flow and ebb with the current.

Dundrennan: Dusk

On the rain-flecked track my footsteps are swallowed
by mist which steams off the loch,
drapes itself around the hills like a sash.
A few sheep on the knolls are still, look almost
painted. Berries on a rowan tree are the only splash
of real colour. A mallard glides through the water,
takes refuge in the rushes.

This is when myth slithers into consciousness.
I wait for the drowned girl to rise
among patches of water-lilies, face
white and bloated, hair tangled and lank.

A sheep bleats, the spell crumbles.
A trick of the weather and light.
I turn back the way I have come,
not quite certain that it means nothing.

Old Year's Night

Stilted laughter and too-loud remarks
attempted a defence against the freezing night.
A heavy torch assisted their clumsy descent
between nettles and dog-roses.

When they heard the sea's sigh, their noise melted
and by the time they moved onto the beach
they had each withdrawn into cocoons of thought.

A battered duffel bag was placed on sand.
Each delved for paper, pens, small white candles,
claimed a position where water withdrew.

Some had only met that evening,
come together to mark that abstract moment
when tradition says the old dies
and the new is given life with a harsh slap.

Kneeling beneath the haloed moon
they wrote out long-considered troubles:
memories that clung to their backs like rucksacks
were folded into careful boats
precisely balanced by candle-masts.

Second-hands sprinted towards midnight.
Shielded matches were struck.
Candles sputtered in the salt-breeze
but shone on, and as the year quietly fell away
the doomed flotilla was launched.

New Year's Day

Imagine snow fell last night.
Imagine fields and hills as still and silent
as a stopped clock. The air is blue, cold:
a cold so thick you could carve your name in it;
even the stream has turned to glass
but the cold doesn't chill the bone as it should
but refreshes, revitalises
like a summer-morning swim.

Snow furs the leafless sycamores,
sharpens the needles of pine and spruce,
rests like a homemade quilt on rocks.
You didn't realise so many shades of white.

Each single blade of grass is in stark relief
so fields and hills look not smothered with snow
but like fields and hills of white, white grass
drawing light from the low white sun
to burn their possibilities onto your retina.

The landscape holds its breath
ready for the coming year to begin its slow drip
like a frozen waterfall beginning to thaw
with the soft chiming of a glass handbell,
or begin like a word you've spoken,
drifting and expanding in a plume of vapour.